God Smiled

written and illustrated
by Dan Foote

FaithKidz®

Equipping Kids for Life

An Imprint of Cook Communications Ministries
Colorado Springs, CO

Faith Parenting Guide

Ages **4-7**

Joy

A Faith Parenting Guide
can be found on page 32.

Additional copies of this book are available from your local bookstore.

If you have enjoyed this book, or if it has impacted your life,
we would like to hear from you.

Please contact us at:
Cook Communications Ministries
4050 Lee Vance View
Colorado Springs, CO 80918
www.cookministries.com

Faith Kidz is an imprint of Cook Communications Ministries
Colorado Springs, Colorado 80918
Cook Communications, Paris, Ontario
Kingsway Communications, Eastbourne, England

First printing, 2005
Manufactured in China.
1 2 3 4 5 6 7 8 9 10 Printing/Year 08 07 06 05

ISBN 078144117X

Editor: Heather Gemmen
Creative Director: Randy Maid
Design Manager: Nancy L. Haskins
Cover Designer: Helen Harrison/YaYe Design
Interior Designer: Patricia Keene

Dedication

To my brothers Dave, Doug, and Darren—for all the many years of laughter and joy and for the constant reminder that God is the author and creator of our mirth.

4

G od smiled.

And his smile floated
like a song on a breeze...

So the ants stopped the march
and praised God with a dance.
The bees sang in harmony
from the hive.

The cricket played along
in his best shirt and pants.
And their music
made the hills come alive!

And the big blue fish smiled...

The big blue fish
bubbled the tune.
The turtles joined in
on a shell.

The frog croaked "Hallelujah"
into a spoon.
And their praise
echoed over the dell.

And the robin smiled...

MUD BATH

The robin sang the song
from high in the sky.
The chipmunk prayed it
deep in the wood.

The cow mooed each note
for the pig in his sty.
And Zeke the dog howled,
"God is so good!"

And the baby smiled...

12

The baby cooed the song while counting her toes. Her brother sprayed it through two missing teeth.

Their mother did a jig while clipping a rose. And their music drifted over the heath.

14

And the chambermaid smiled...

The chambermaid skipped
and sang over the moat.
The prince plucked the tune
on his lyre.

The queen's heart leapt
at the sound of each note.
And the song bounced
from dungeon to spire.

18

And the king smiled...

20

The king sang, "Praise God!"
from high in his tower.
The pines swayed in rhythm
in the forest.

The fields made an orchestra
of every flower
while the brook gurgled
the wonderful chorus.

And the mountains smiled...

The mountains majestically
lifted their praise.
The oceans took the song
out to sea.

The thunderclouds flashed
for all to amaze—
and remind us how
mighty God can be.

And the moon smiled....

The moon glowed the melody
out into space.
The sun whistled and burned
ever more bright.

The stars twinkled the tune
like diamond lace.
And the whole universe
praised God with their light.

And the angel smiled...

The angel crooned
for all of heaven to hear.
The band joined in
on the third beat.

They ended the song
to a thunderous cheer.
And the tune of praise
was placed gently at God's feet.

And God smiled...

God Smiled

Life Issue: I want my children to experience
the joy of God through his wonderful creation.
Spiritual Building Block: Joy

Use the following activities to help your children experience joy through God's creation.

Sight:

Go outside with your children, whether at a local park or in your backyard, and ask them to show you things that God has created that make them happy. Talk to them about all the variety in God's creation and how it makes the world more exciting.

Sound:

Ask your children to sit quietly and listen to God's creation. Ask each of them what they hear— leaves blowing, crickets chirping, birds singing, and so on. Talk about how each noise they hear is another part of God's creation voicing its love and happiness for him. Ask your children to name some ways they can voice their love and happiness to God.

Touch:

Read together Psalm 148, on which **God Smiled** is based. Talk about how it is like a song. It details how everything in God's creation, from the smallest to the grandest, sings God's praises. Help your children also use songs and nature as a vehicle for praising God. Take your children for a hike through the woods or a walk through your neighborhood. Let them pick favorite praise songs to sing together as you walk. Remind your children how God loves to see us happy and praising him.